Meat and Two Veg

A play

Paul Beard

Samuel French—London
New York-Toronto-Hollywood

CHARACTERS

Margaret
Arthur
Albert

The action of the play takes place in the living-room of a South Coast retirement bungalow

Time: early summer evening

COPYRIGHT INFORMATION
(See also page ii)

MEAT AND TWO VEG

The living-room of Margaret's and Arthur's South Coast retirement bungalow. There are french windows UC; DL is a door which leads to the kitchen. On stage is a dining table, three chairs and a waste-paper basket. (Other setting at Director's discretion)

Margaret enters and lays three place settings on the table

Arthur enters UC. He is carrying some runner beans. A tape measure slightly protrudes from his pocket

Margaret (*slightly annoyed*) I said French beans—not runner beans.

Arthur I've picked them now.

Margaret You can't serve *coq au vin* with runner beans.

Arthur They're the same colour.

Margaret It's a French dish. It should be French beans.

Arthur The chicken's English. You bought it at Sainsbury's.

Margaret Place of birth is irrelevant, Arthur. The recipe just calls for chicken.

Arthur If it's a French dish, it should be a French chicken.

Margaret I can disguise the chicken.

Arthur Not with a beret, striped shirt and a string of onions around its neck, I hope?

Margaret With the sauce. Now hurry up. Albert will be here in a minute.

Arthur Why can't he eat at his own house for a change?

Margaret He's lonely. It can't be nice for him now that Enid's gone.

Arthur You make it sound as if she's dead. She's left him, that's all. I would have done the same, if I had to live with him. He can be very difficult at times.

Margaret It's his age.

Arthur We're his age. We're not difficult.

Margaret There must be more to it than that. If all women left their husbands just because they were being difficult, the divorce rate would be much higher.

Arthur He's never said *why* she left him.

Margaret Perhaps you should ask him.

Arthur You ask him.

Margaret He's your friend.

Arthur He's a neighbour, that's all.

Margaret He probably thinks we don't care.

Arthur I don't. If he weren't so difficult she wouldn't have gone.

Margaret I wonder where she is.

Arthur Can't have gone far. She's left all her clothes behind. I noticed the piles of ironing when I went round yesterday to borrow some potting compost.

Margaret Did you have a word with him about those smelly bonfires?

Arthur Not yet.

Margaret It's getting so I can't hang out the washing. One of your best nylon shirts has got a burn hole in it and I've got smuts all over my smalls.

Arthur I don't know why he needs to have so many. I'll speak to him tonight.

Margaret Are you going to get the French beans?

Arthur What do you want me to do with these?

Margaret You could try sticking them back on with Blu-Tack, or you could try sticking them where the sun doesn't shine. Failing that, I would put them in the vegetable rack with the ones you picked yesterday and the day before and the day before that.

Arthur Does it have to be *coq au vin*? Couldn't you change it to chicken in red wine sauce and serve it with runner beans?

Margaret Nobody likes runner beans.

Arthur We've got plenty.

Margaret We've always got plenty. The freezer is full to the brim with runner beans. Last year's runner beans, the year before that's runner beans—in fact, we've even got runner beans labelled nineteen seventy-six.

Arthur (*proudly*) Best crop ever, '76.

Margaret (*resignedly*) Will there ever be a year when we don't grow runner beans?

Arthur Everybody grows runner beans. What would happen if nobody grew runner beans?

Margaret We'd have an empty freezer for a start. Are you going to pick me some French beans, or not?

Arthur You don't want these?

Margaret Give me the beans, Arthur.

Arthur (*pleased*) I knew you'd see sense. (*He hands her the beans*)

She throws them in the waste bin

You are so wasteful. They'll be ruined now. I could have blanched those and put them in the freezer.

Margaret (*snapping*) There's no room in the freezer. It's full up with your runner beans.

Arthur Perhaps I should consider exporting them to surrounding neighbourhoods.

Margaret Perhaps you should consider not growing any more.

Arthur You can't have a vegetable garden without runner beans. This is England—the home of the humble runner bean. (*He picks a bean out of the bin and measures it*) Look at that. Eight inches of prime runner bean. Wasted. Months of careful nurturing gone.

Margaret It's a bean, for God's sake.

Arthur No. It's a runner bean. My runner bean. I've watched this grow from a single purple bean. Carefully stored in the dark until all danger of frost has passed. Watching. Waiting. Until that glorious moment as the first pair of tiny leaves break through the surface. From its first appearance in the world I've cared for it. Protected it from slugs. I've even held conversations with it. It's my bean.

Margaret (*unsympathetic*) We should have had children.

Arthur They're all my beans.

Margaret You would have made a wonderful father.

Arthur (*to the beans*) "Mary Mary quite contrary. How does your garden grow…"

Margaret With runner beans and runner beans and runner beans all in a row. If I hear the word bean mentioned once more this evening, I will not be held responsible for my actions.

Arthur I'll dispose of the…

Margaret I'm warning you, Arthur.

Arthur The *phaseolus multiflorus*.

Margaret Thank you.

Arthur Will you be wanting the long tubular green things. The *phaseolus vulgaris*. The haricot vert'. The…

Margaret …The French beans, yes.

Arthur You said the 'b' word. That's not fair.

Margaret (*snapping*) I'll use more than the 'b' word if you don't get yourself into the garden and pick me some French…

Arthur Beans?

Margaret screams and throws a place mat at Arthur as he exits UC

She continues to set the table

Albert enters UC. *He carries a small brown bag containing runner beans*

Albert Being difficult, is he?

Margaret Is he ever anything else, Albert?

Albert It's his age.

Margaret We're his age. We're not difficult.

Albert He should be careful. You could go next.

Margaret If I was going to leave Arthur because he was difficult, I would have left him the moment he retired.

Albert Mmmm, something smells good.

Margaret *Coq au vin.*
Albert My favourite.
Margaret Everything's your favourite, Albert.
Albert I've bought you a little present.
Margaret You shouldn't.
Albert Perfect for *coq au vin*.
Margaret After dinner mints?
Albert (*producing a bag*) Runner beans.
Margaret Oh.
Albert (*proudly*) Ten inch beauties. Organic. None of that fertilized rubbish you get at the supermarket.
Margaret (*lying*) Perfect.
Albert Better than those rotten French ones, don't you think?
Margaret (*lying*) Much better.
Albert I wouldn't mind betting that French freezers are full up with the things. Can't give them away over there. They'd give their hind teeth to be able to get hold of these beauties.
Margaret I'll just pop through and put them on to boil.

Margaret exits DL

Arthur enters UC. *He is carrying some purple French beans*

Arthur I've got them.
Albert So you have. Are those French beans?
Arthur Yes.
Albert Not very big, are they?
Arthur Big enough.
Albert They're the wrong colour.
Arthur They change colour when you cook them.
Albert Bit pointless. Typical French. Can't even get the colour of a green bean right. Probably an EEC directive.
Arthur I'd better get these through to Margaret. She's in a bit of a mood.
Albert Being difficult, is she?
Arthur Is she ever anything else?

Albert It's her age.

Arthur We're her age. We're not difficult.

Albert It's probably a womanly thing. Something hormonal. How are your runners coming along?

Arthur Mainly ten inch. A few elevens.

Albert No twelves?

Arthur One or two. You?

Albert The smallest is about fourteen.

Arthur I always think they start to lose their flavour after twelve.

Albert Not mine.

Arthur Go a bit stringy.

Albert Not my babies. I could let you in on a few trade secrets if yours are a bit tough.

Arthur Mine? I wasn't talking about mine. I was talking in general. My beans are never tough.

Albert I've forgotten the wine. I'll just pop back and get it.

Arthur We do have wine.

Albert I always bring the wine. Can't expect to be fed for nothing.

Albert exits UC

Arthur (*calling after him*) My beans are never tough.

Margaret enters DL

Margaret Where's Albert?

Arthur (*sulking*) I've killed him. He said my beans were tough.

Margaret He's just being difficult. It's his age. Where's he gone?

Arthur He's gone to get the wine.

Margaret (*worried*) Oh, no.

Arthur I hope it's not the rhubarb '82. The last time I had that, I had the runs for a week.

Margaret I lost half a stone.

Arthur Perhaps he should market it as a miracle diet.

Margaret Or a laxative.

Arthur I've got the beans.

Margaret Oh.

Arthur You do want them, don't you?

Margaret Well…

Arthur He's given you some of his French beans, hasn't he?

Margaret No, it's just…

Arthur They're bigger than mine. Is that what it is?

Margaret Size isn't everything, Arthur.

Arthur No? Then why are you using *his* French beans?

Margaret Runner beans.

Arthur What?

Margaret He's a guest. He offered.

Arthur He did that on purpose. What size are they?

Margaret What is this preoccupation with size, Arthur?

Arthur (*sulking*) Well, I'm not eating them and that's that. I want French beans. *Coq au vin* is a French dish—it should be French beans. You said so.

Margaret He would have been offended if I turned them down.

Arthur I'm just your husband. I don't count.

Margaret He's a guest.

Arthur He practically lives here.

Margaret That's not fair, Arthur. We both agreed it would be a neighbourly thing to do until Enid came back.

Arthur What if she never comes back?

Margaret Of course she'll come back.

Arthur He fancies you.

Margaret Don't be silly.

Arthur I've seen him looking at you.

Margaret He doesn't.

Arthur He's always had an eye for you—even before Enid left.

Margaret Arthur, you are making a mountain out of a molehill. There's no need to be jealous. He's just a friend. My friend and your friend. We're all friends.

Arthur (*sulking*) I don't like runner beans.

Margaret I'll cook your beans. They're probably bigger than his anyway.

Margaret exits DL

Albert enters UC. *He is carrying a bottle of wine and some large French beans*

Albert Now, these are what you call French beans. They're the right colour for a start. What would you say—seven inches?

Arthur Six at the most.

Albert Where's your tape.

Arthur I've lost it.

Albert What's that hanging out of your pocket then?

Arthur So that's where it is. I've been looking for that for days.

Albert Let's have it then.

Arthur So they're sevens. Size isn't everything. You forget about things like texture and taste.

Albert (*toying with a bean*) Good colour. Good texture. Perfect taste.

Arthur Shall I open the wine?

Albert Rhubarb '82. Perfect for *coq au vin*.

Arthur Couldn't we have the apple '86?

Albert This is Margaret's favourite.

Arthur I've lost the corkscrew.

Albert Shall I fetch mine?

Arthur No. I've got a bottle of dandelion '94 in the fridge. It's got a screw cap and it's in a much bigger bottle.

Margaret enters DL *with a corkscrew*

Margaret You'll need the corkscrew, Arthur.

Arthur Rhubarb '82.

Margaret Oh.

Albert (*proudly*) A classic year for rhubarb.

Margaret (*lying*) Perfect for *coq au vin*.

Arthur (*under his breath*) Judas.

Albert Shall I do the honour?

Arthur I can manage.

Margaret It's Albert's wine. He should open the bottle.

Arthur He always opens the bottle.

Margaret It's his wine, Arthur.

Arthur It was my rhubarb.

Albert I gave you some carrots for that rhubarb.

Arthur I couldn't use them. They were too small.

Albert They were not small. I don't grow small.

Arthur Your onions are small.

Albert They're shallots.

Margaret (*snapping*) Will you two stop bickering about the size of your vegetables.

Arthur

Albert

Margaret Fine. Now, sit down and I'll serve dinner.

Arthur (*sulking*) No beans for me.

Albert (*sulking*) Nor me.

Margaret (*resignedly*) Fine. No beans for anybody then.

Margaret exits DL

Albert They make good compost—beans.

Arthur The best. Perfect start for next year's crop.

Albert Have you had your catalogue through yet?

Arthur No.

Albert Got mine today. I could get it after dinner if you like.

Arthur Any new varieties?

Albert Plenty.

Margaret enters with three plates of coq au vin *and places them on the table*

Margaret *Coq au vin* for three—no beans.

They sit down to eat

Albert Mmmm, that looks nice.

Arthur Something's missing. Needs something green to set it off.

Albert This chicken is superb, Margaret.

Margaret Thank you, Albert.

Albert These your potatoes, Arthur?

Arthur Why?

Albert Nice taste.

Arthur Not too small?

Albert I expect they were larger before they were peeled.

Arthur Huge. One of them weighed at least three stone.

Albert I always find they lose their taste if they're too big. These are nice though.

Margaret I bought them at Sainsbury's.

Arthur Why didn't you use mine?

Margaret They've gone green.

Albert You should store them in a sack in the dark, Arthur.

Arthur You could have cut the green bits off.

Margaret They taste funny.

Arthur They're organic. They're supposed to taste different.

Margaret I prefer the proper ones. They cook better.

Arthur What have you done with my potatoes?

Margaret I put them on the compost heap.

Albert Makes great compost—potatoes.

Arthur (*sulking*) I'm not eating these. They could be full of chemicals.

Albert More wine, Margaret?

Margaret No, thank you, Albert. I've got a bit of an upset stomach.

Arthur You won't have a stomach if you drink more than one glass of that.

Albert It's your rhubarb.

Arthur There was nothing wrong with the rhubarb. Best crop ever, '82.

Albert (*putting down his knife and fork*) That was wonderful, Margaret. Arthur, you don't know how lucky you are having someone like Margaret to look after you.

Arthur At least I'd be able to fend for myself if my wife went off and left me.

Albert What do you mean by…

Margaret …Is there any news of Enid? It's been nearly two months now.

Albert (*sadly*) Six weeks and four days.

Arthur (*sarcastically*) Mark it on the calendar, did you?

Albert It was the day I planted the brussels. I was a bit on edge. You know how it is when you're transplanting them from seed trays, Arthur.

Margaret Did she say where she was going? Or why she was leaving?

Albert You wouldn't think it possible that a woman could be jealous of a marrow, would you?

Arthur They don't understand.

Albert Huge, she was.

Margaret Enid was never huge.

Albert The marrow. Perfect colouring. A prize winner, if ever there was one.

Margaret (*sympathetically*) She'll be back.

Albert I've only the one photograph.

Margaret There's plenty on your mantelpiece.

Albert Not of the marrow.

Margaret Enid.

Albert Oh, I've got loads of photos of Enid. Only one of the marrow though.

Arthur Can't enter a photo in the show can you? Shame really, I was looking forward to a bit of competition this year. Gloria is coming on a treat.

Margaret Who's Gloria?

Arthur My marrow. Grown three centimetres since I last measured her.

Albert Wouldn't have beaten Cynthia.

Margaret What happened to it?

Albert On the compost heap.

Margaret Why?

Albert Enid hit me over the head with it.

Arthur Makes good compost—marrow.

Albert She wanted to cook her.

Arthur Murder!

Margaret It's only a marrow.

Arthur They'll never understand.

Albert Plenty of others, but she wanted Cynthia.

Arthur Grounds for divorce, that. Unreasonable behaviour.

Albert (*sadly*) I do miss her.

Margaret (*sympathetically*) She'll be back.

Albert There'll never be another Cynthia.

Margaret (*resignedly*) I'll get the pudding.

Margaret exits DL

Albert When I opened the packet of seeds, I knew straight away which one she was. She had a darker complexion than the others. The ridges of the skin formed a perfect smile. It was as if she was pleading with me to take special care of her.

Arthur She sounds wonderful.

Albert Would you like to see the photo? I can get the catalogue at the same time.

Arthur OK. It would have been nicer to see her before she passed away though.

Albert exits UC

Margaret enters DL *with three plates of apple crumble*

Margaret Where's he gone now?

Arthur To get the photograph.

Margaret Of the marrow?

Arthur He's depressed.

Margaret His wife's left him and he's grieving over a marrow?

Arthur A prize marrow. There's a difference.

Margaret A marrow is a marrow, Arthur. He needs counselling, if you ask me.

Arthur Grief counselling?

Margaret Full blown psychiatric treatment seems to fit the bill. Perhaps you could ask for a reduced rate and go with him.

Arthur I've never grieved over a marrow.

Margaret You cried when the blossom fell off your apple tree.

Arthur I've never had to buy apples before. What's for pudding?

Margaret Apple crumble.

Arthur You can be very cruel sometimes, Margaret.

Margaret Albert gave them to me.

Arthur Big, are they?

Margaret About average. Have you had a word with him about the bonfires yet?

Arthur Not yet.

Margaret You promised.

Arthur We all need to have bonfires this time of year.

Margaret Not every night. Not when they smell as bad as his.

Arthur It's probably all the chemicals.

Margaret I thought he was organic?

Arthur He says he is, but you don't get your vegetables as big as his without cheating.

Margaret Perhaps that's where you're going wrong.

Arthur There's nothing wrong with Mother Nature. If man was supposed to have a twelve inch cucumber, we would have twelve inch cucumbers without resorting to artificial stimulants.

Margaret Albert doesn't seem the type of person who cheats.

Arthur He plays Frank Sinatra to his courgettes. I caught him. He pretended he was just listening to the tape but he never fooled me. Artificial stimulants, see. Saves hours and hours of endless conversations with them.

Margaret Perhaps we should buy him his greatest hits for Christmas.

Arthur You shouldn't encourage him.

Margaret I don't.

Arthur He was leering at you over the chicken.

Margaret He wasn't.

Arthur He's always leering at you.

Margaret He doesn't. You're just being silly.

Arthur Don't think I don't know what's going on. You hardly ever wore a dress before Enid left.

Margaret I did.

Arthur You're flaunting yourself at him. He's trying to seduce you with the offer of bigger vegetables.

Margaret Yours are plenty big enough for me, Arthur. You're imagining it. Stop being silly.

Arthur He's probably killed her.

Margaret Who?

Arthur Enid. He's probably chopped her up into little pieces. He was a butcher, you know. That's why he's been having so many bonfires. Getting rid of the evidence.

Margaret Stop it, Arthur.

Arthur Makes good compost—ashes. You're being wooed by a wife murderer.

Albert enters UC. *He carries a photograph and a catalogue*

Albert Sorry I was so long. Had to light a bonfire.

Arthur and Margaret exchange glances

Margaret I'll get the custard.

Margaret exits DL

Albert Are those my apples?

Arthur Apparently.

Albert Shame about your blossom.

Arthur *I* don't have a tape recorder.

Albert What?

Arthur Nothing.

Albert You'll like these. New variety.

Arthur (*sarcastically*) Sinatra's, are they?

Albert Egremont Russet.

Margaret enters DL, *carrying a jug of custard*

Margaret Custard, Arthur?

Arthur Lots.

Margaret pours the custard into Arthur's dish

Albert Just a little for me, please.

Margaret slams the jug in front of Albert and sits

You'll like these, Margaret. New variety. Organic.
Margaret (*offhand*) I've gone off apples, thank you.
Albert Shame to waste them.
Arthur Makes good compost—apples.
Margaret Not as good as *ash*, though.
Albert True.
Margaret *Burnt* ash.
Albert (*laughing*) Is there any other kind?
Margaret (*curtly*) You should know.
Arthur Is that the new catalogue?
Albert Arrived today.
Margaret If you two are going to talk vegetables for the rest of the
  evening, I'll watch TV upstairs. Bonfires, Arthur.

  Margaret exits DL

Albert Is it my imagination, or has Margaret's mood taken a turn
  for the worse?
Arthur You've upset her. She doesn't like you staring at her.
Albert I don't.
Arthur She's an attractive woman.
Albert I wouldn't stare at another man's wife, Arthur.
Arthur Nice legs.
Albert True.
Arthur You've noticed then?
Albert Only in passing. I wasn't staring, Arthur. Honest.
Arthur Just don't go getting any ideas, that's all. I don't mind the
  odd sharing of tools, but she's my wife. You never caught me
  staring at Enid, did you?
Albert Nobody would stare at Enid.
Arthur Enough said. Any idea where she is?
Albert She's probably at her brother's in Porthcawl. Grows good
  runner beans. Hopeless at leeks, mind.

Arthur Margaret's asked me to have a word with you about your
bonfires.
Albert Oh yes?
Arthur You've been having them almost every night and they've
started to smell a bit.
Albert That'll be the bones.
Arthur Bones?
Albert I get them from the butcher. Best natural fertiliser you can
get. Blood and bone. I can let you have some, if you like?
Arthur Well, if you're sure.
Albert Got plenty. Whole sack of the things in the garage.
Arthur I'd have to burn them down when Margaret was out.
Albert We could do it together.

Margaret enters UC. *She is now wearing trousers and holds a
small piece of bone behind her back*

I thought you were upstairs watching TV?
Margaret Nothing on.
Arthur You've changed.
Margaret I was cold.
Arthur What were you doing in the garden?
Margaret Ehm … just getting some fresh air.
Albert You just said you were cold.
Margaret Ehm … I was then… I'm not now. Albert, your bonfire
looks like it might get out of control.
Albert Can't do any damage. It's not close to anything that could
catch light.
Margaret The wind has changed direction. Your runner beans look
a bit singed.
Albert Better check. Peace of mind and all that. Won't be long.

Albert exits UC

Margaret (*producing the bone*) Look.
Arthur What is it?

Margaret Part of a bone. I found it by the fire.

Arthur What were you doing in Albert's garden'?

Margaret Looking for evidence. Are we, or are we not, living next door to a wife murderer?

Arthur Of course we're not. I was joking.

Margaret What about this? (*She hands him the bone*)

Arthur It's a bone.

Margaret It's Enid.

Arthur I can't see the resemblance somehow.

Margaret How can you sit there and make jokes about the mutilation of our next door neighbour?

Arthur It's an animal bone. He gets them from the butcher.

Margaret And you believed him?

Arthur Of course.

Margaret He's hardly likely to tell you that he's spent the last six nights cutting up and burning his wife, is he?

Arthur (*examining the bone*) It's still got a piece of flesh attached to it.

Margaret Don't, Arthur. It's macabre.

Arthur (*breaking a piece off*) I could try tasting it.

Margaret Don't be disgusting.

Arthur (*nibbling at it*) Tastes like pork. (*He offers her the bone*) Here, what do you think?

Margaret If you think I'm tucking in to my next door neighbour, you've got another think coming.

Arthur (*nibbling at it*) Could be lamb. It's tender enough.

Margaret How can you sit there and eat Enid? You are sick, Arthur. I'm calling the police.

Arthur Don't be silly, Margaret. What are you going to say? "Sorry to trouble you officer, only I think my husband's eating my next door neighbour".

Margaret We've got to do something. He's killed her. I want you to search through his compost heap.

Arthur I can't go meddling about in another man's compost. It wouldn't be right. He'd think it was industrial espionage. The composition of a man's compost heap is a trade secret. I'd be thrown out of the Horticultural Society.

Margaret Please, Arthur. I won't be able to sleep knowing that Enid might be rotting away amongst the household waste.

Arthur You're being silly.

Margaret You've seen the way he looks at me. I could be next.

Arthur You didn't tread on any of his vegetables while you were in the garden, did you?

Margaret (*defensively*) It was an accident. I tripped over a watering can and fell into the *petit pois*.

Arthur Not his prized *pisum sativum macrocarpoums*?

Margaret We could blame it on the cats.

Arthur It'd take a pack of Bengal tigers to create the kind of damage you've probably done.

Margaret (*embarrassed*) I think I trod on a few onions as well.

Arthur Well, that's it then. It'll be *Friday the Thirteenth*, part sixty-four, all over again. He's probably out there now, slaying half the neighbourhood with a Dutch hoe.

Margaret Don't make such a fuss. They're only vegetables.

Arthur The *petit pois* were a particular favourite with Albert. Always got a good crop.

Margaret Well, he's got a mange-tout patch now. Are you going to search the compost or not?

Arthur You're wrong about this, you know.

Margaret I'm not. I can feel it in my…

Arthur …Bones?

Margaret Poor Enid.

Arthur You'll have to keep him in here if I do it. I don't want him catching me dirty-handed.

Margaret How?

Arthur Talk to him.

Margaret About what?

Arthur Anything. Vegetables. I don't know. Anything. Put your dress back on. Flaunt yourself at him.

Margaret I couldn't.

Arthur It won't do any harm. Just let him look at your legs for a bit. That should keep him busy.

Margaret On your head be it, Arthur.

Margaret exits DL

Albert enters UC

Albert Bloody kids!

Arthur What?

Albert The little bleeders have wrecked my *petit pois* patch and kicked my onions all over the place. If I ever got hold of them I'd give them what for, I can tell you.

Arthur Kids, eh?

Albert It's probably those Thompson twins from number seven. They should have been put down at birth those two. I knew they'd be trouble from the day they moved in. Garden full of gnomes. Not a vegetable in sight.

Arthur How's the bonfire?

Albert Flog 'em, that's what I say.

Arthur They're girls, Albert.

Albert You should see the state of those poor onions.

Arthur How's the bonfire?

Albert The wind must have dropped. There's nothing wrong with it. Where's Margaret?

Arthur Gone up to change.

Margaret enters DL. *She is wearing an ankle length skirt*

Margaret Could you fetch me some runner beans from the garden, Arthur?

Arthur There's plenty in the freezer.

Margaret I need them fresh.

Arthur Why?

Margaret From the garden.

Albert I'll fetch you some of mine if you want.

Margaret I'd prefer Arthur's.

Albert Mine are much bigger.

Margaret I need them small. I'm making ratatouille.

Albert You need French beans for that.

Margaret It's the English version. Off you go, Arthur.
Arthur Where?
Margaret (*angrily*) In the garden!
Arthur You're wrong about this, you know.
Albert Possibly not. Should be quite nice—ratatouille with runner
   beans.
Margaret Garden, Arthur.
Arthur (*resignedly*) Won't be long.

   Arthur exits UC

Margaret He can be so difficult sometimes.
Albert It's a cruel thing, old age.
Margaret Anything you fancy, Albert?
Albert What?
Margaret In the new catalogue.
Albert For a moment there I...
Margaret ...Yes?
Albert That you were offering me something else.
Margaret Tea?
Albert (*disappointed*) No, thank you.

Short pause

Margaret Nice weather we're having.
Albert Could do with a drop more rain.
Margaret Yes.
Albert Never had these droughts when the water companies were
   in public ownership.
Margaret No.

Short pause

Albert He's taking his time. Shall I go and see where he's got to?
Margaret There's no need, Albert.
Albert (*rising*) It's no trouble, Margaret.

Margaret stands and raises her skirt above her knees

Margaret Do you think I've got attractive knees, Albert?
Albert (*sitting and looking away*) Don't, Margaret. I don't know where to look.
Margaret At my knees.
Albert (*staring at her knees*) I wouldn't want to be accused of staring.
Margaret Did Enid have nice knees, Albert?
Albert Did? Why did you say, "did"?
Margaret Ehm, I meant "does". Of course I meant "does". What on earth made me say "did", it's not as if she's dead or anything, is it?
Albert Are you feeling all right, Margaret?
Margaret Fine. Just fine.
Albert (*rising*) I'll just go and…

Margaret moves in to him

Margaret Do you think I've got nice eyes, Albert?
Albert It's hard to tell, really. I'm long-sighted. You'll have to move back a bit for me to see.

Arthur enters UC

Arthur (*coughing*) Not interrupting anything, am I?
Albert (*guiltily*) No, no. Margaret had something in her eye, that's all.
Margaret Have you got the beans?
Arthur Beans?
Margaret You went into the garden to pick some beans for the ratatouille, remember?
Albert I'll get you some of mine, Margaret. It'll be a lot quicker.

Albert exits UC

Arthur He probably thinks I've gone ga-ga now.

Margaret Did you find anything?

Arthur I think I disturbed a hedgehog.

Margaret Enid!

Arthur Of course I didn't find Enid. You're wrong about this, you know.

Margaret Will you stop saying that? I'm right. I know I'm right. I just hope you did a proper job of it out there.

Arthur I've destroyed his compost heap. His pride and joy. He's been building that for over two years.

Margaret Did you look in the potting shed?

Arthur You never asked me to look in the potting shed.

Margaret Use your common sense, Arthur. If she's not in the compost heap, she must be in the potting shed.

Arthur She's at her brother's.

Margaret I want you to have a look in the potting shed, please, Arthur.

Arthur I can't keep going in and out to the garden or he really will think I've gone ga-ga.

Margaret Potting shed or I call the police.

Arthur Right. Potting shed it is. But if she's not in there, that's it. Agreed?

Margaret What about the greenhouse?

Arthur Agreed?

Margaret Agreed.

Albert enters UC. *He is carrying some runner beans*

Albert I'll bet you haven't got one as big as this, Arthur.

Margaret This is becoming very personal, Albert. The pair of you should be grateful you've got anything at all. This competition about size is in such bad taste, considering some Third World countries can't grow enough crops of any size to feed their children.

Albert Sorry, Margaret. Just a bit of harmless fun. Nothing meant by it.

Margaret Enough said. I've made my point. Off you go, Arthur.

Albert Where's he going now?

Margaret I need French beans after all. I had another look at the recipe and it said, "Under no circumstances use runner beans".

Albert I've picked these now.

Margaret Don't worry. I'll blanch them and put them in the freezer. Off you go, Arthur.

Arthur exits UC

Slight pause

How long have we known you now, Albert?

Albert Years.

Margaret Would you say we were good friends?

Albert I'd like to think so.

Margaret Close friends?

Albert Almost family.

Short pause

Margaret You used to be a butcher, didn't you?

Albert A long time ago.

Margaret I couldn't cope with something like that. Blood everywhere. Lumps of raw meat all over the place.

Albert You get used to it.

Short pause

Margaret I saw a film once about a plane crash. The survivors had to eat the flesh of the dead to survive. One of them said it tasted just like pork.

Albert Really?

Margaret Although, apparently, it was so tender it could have been lamb.

Albert Closer to pork, I would have thought. White meat, you see.

Short pause

Margaret There shouldn't be any secrets between close friends, I
    always say.
Albert No.

Short pause

Margaret Have you heard the expression, "Confession is good for
    the soul", Albert?
Albert You know, don't you?
Margaret Do I?
Albert I was provoked. She deserved it. I was at my wit's end.
Margaret I'll have to call the police, Albert. Friend or no friend.
Albert Not the police, Margaret. That's not fair. You should see
    what she did to my compost heap.
Margaret What?
Albert Two years work. Wrecked.
Margaret What are you talking about?
Albert I threw one of my pumpkins at her. Hit her right between
    the eyes.
Margaret Enid?
Albert No. One of those girls from number seven. Don't ask me
    which one, they both look the same, only one of them is wearing
    a pumpkin on her head at the present. I'm not sorry either. Call
    the police if you want. I'll take my chance with a judge and jury
    any day.
Margaret Oh.
Albert You won't turn me in, will you, Margaret? Not for
    something like this, surely.
Margaret Not for something like that—no. (*She pauses*) What
    about Enid?
Albert What about her?
Margaret We know what's happened.
Albert I told you what happened. She hit me over the head with
    Cynthia and left.
Margaret Without her clothes?
Albert Without anything.

Margaret And the bonfires?

Albert Yes, I'm sorry about that. Don't worry, I've only got a few
more bones left.

Margaret How could you, Albert?

Albert It's the best way to do it. Burn them down. Makes good
compost.

Margaret It's not proper. I think we should call the police, don't
you?

Albert It's hardly a crime, Margaret.

Margaret Of course it's a crime. We know. We know what's on
your bonfires. We know where she is. Enid is——

Arthur enters UC

Arthur I've found her. I've found Enid in the garden.

Margaret Oh my God. (*She faints and falls to the floor*)

Arthur She was looking for you, Albert. She's brought you back
some runner beans from her brother's.

CURTAIN

FURNITURE AND PROPERTY LIST

On stage: Dining table. *On it:* 3 place settings
               3 matching dining chairs
               Waste paper basket

Off stage: Runner beans (**Arthur**)
               Brown paper bag containing runner beans (**Albert**)
               Purple French beans (**Arthur**)
               Bottle of wine, large French beans (**Albert**)
               Corkscrew (**Margaret**)
               3 plates of *coq au vin* (**Margaret**)
               3 plates of apple crumble (**Margaret**)
               Photograph, catalogue (**Albert**)
               Jug of custard (**Margaret**)
               Small piece of bone (**Margaret**)
               Runner beans (**Albert**)

Personal: **Arthur**: dressmaker's tape

LIGHTING PLOT

To open: Effect of early summer evening

*No cue*s

EFFECTS PLOT

No cues

Printed by
The Kingfisher Press, London NW10 6UG